Because I Am Human

BECAUSE I AM HUMAN

Leo Buscaglia, Ph.D.

photography
Bruce Ferguson

Published by
Charles B. Slack, Inc.

Distributed by
Holt, Rinehart and Winston

This book is dedicated
to David (age 3)
and Christina (age 2)
who started the
celebration and to all
those who want to join in.

BECAUSE I AM HUMAN is a celebration! A celebration of the small but wonderful things we can do, because we are human, which are often taken for granted.

The concept of the book was suggested by a four-year-old child named David. (Why does it always take children to remind us of what is most essential?) David's parents and I were on an educational project with the Sioux Indians in South Dakota. One afternoon we were bumping along on a small road crossing the Badlands. We were discussing the many things we were doing, all of which we felt were enormously significant. I noticed that David, all but ignored, was listening attentively. Seeing this error, I attempted to include him.

"David, you've heard what we are doing. Tell us—what can *you* do"?

Without a moment's hesitation he answered with great pride, "Lots o' things."

"Like what?" I prodded.

"I can spit!"

That *was* indeed a wonder! I, who had worked with cerebral palsied individuals, knew how many years it could take to teach this very basic skill.

"And what else?"

"I can walk."

This was particularly poignant for me who had just recently recovered from several months immobility caused by a ruptured spinal disc.

"I can hug. I can cry. I can roll in the grass."

...and on he went.

How wonderful, I thought. Perhaps we need to be reminded from time to time that much of the joy of being human comes from staying in touch with the little wonders, those abilities most of us are given at birth and which we fail to appreciate until they are lost. So this book.

I hope you will celebrate with David and me by adding your own very human accomplishments to our list so that we may all continually remind each other of the wonder which is ours BECAUSE WE ARE HUMAN.

The Author

Because I Am
Human There Are
So Many Wonderful
Things I Can Do...

I Can Smell A Flower...

I Can Hug...

I Can Roll Down A Hill...

I Can Go To Sleep When I'm Tired...

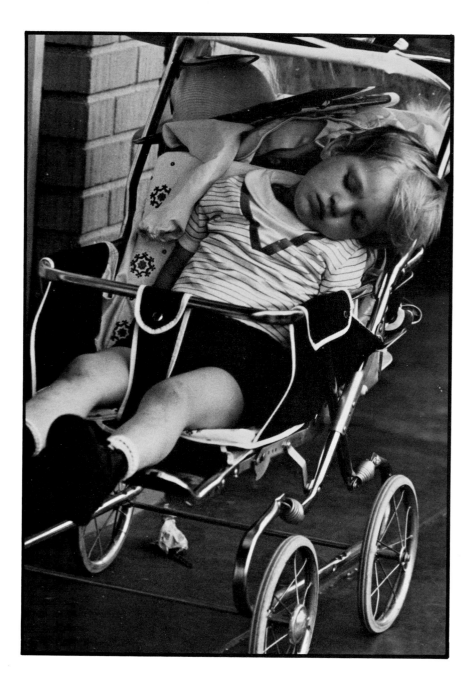

I Can Hold Hands...

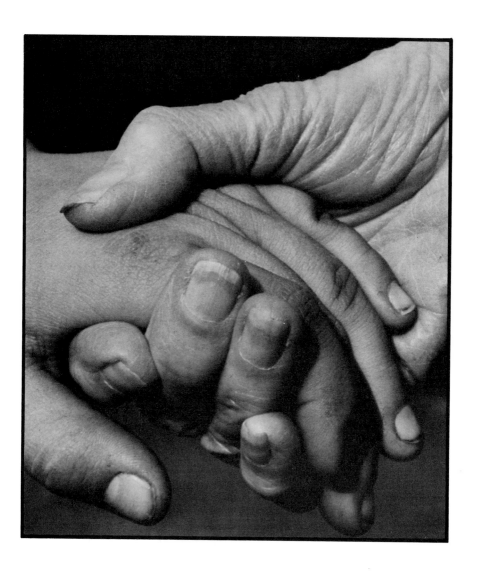

I Can Chew Five Sticks
Of Bubble Gum All At Once...

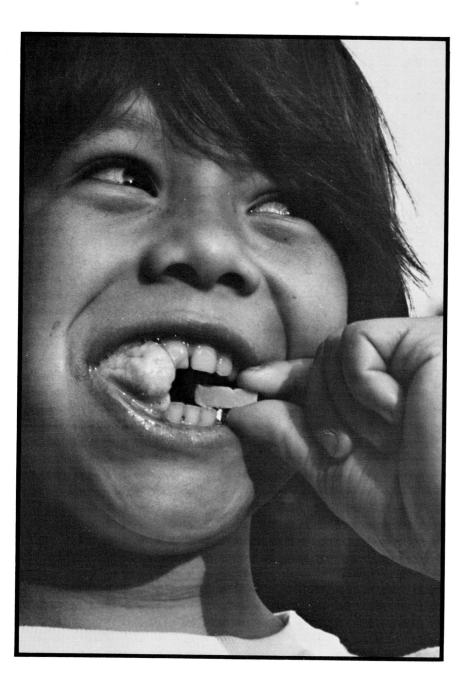

I Can Fall Down
And Not Even Cry...

I Can Look Out A Window...

I Can Believe In Unicorns...

I Can Climb A Tree...

I Can Lie Face Down In The Grass...

I Can Suck Juicy Oranges...

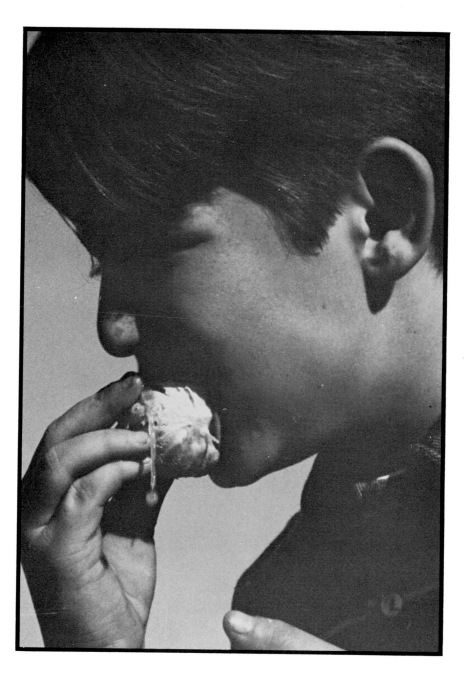

I Can Climb A Mountain...

I Can Listen To A Stream...

I Can Wash My
Feet In Cold Water...

I Can Make A Wish...

I Can Do Things For Myself...

I Can Count Raindrops...

I Can Smile...

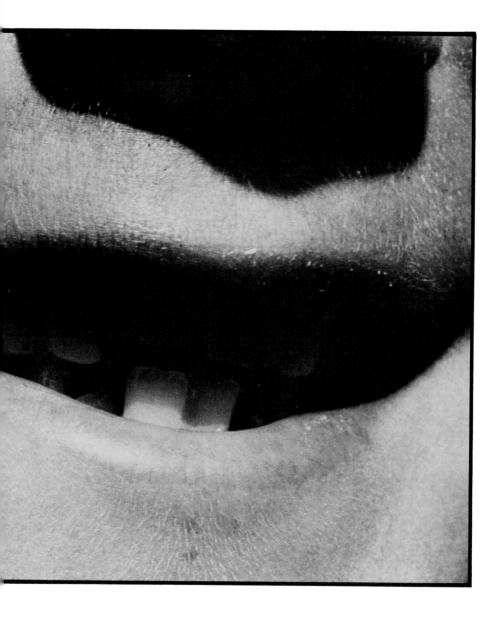

I Can Feel Soft Things...

I Can Put My Finger In My Nose...

I Can Kiss Someone ...

I Can Tickle...

I Can Feel Happy...

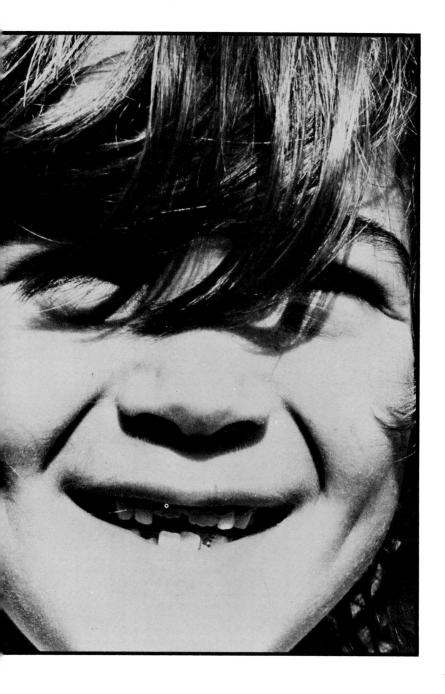

I Can Let The Wind
Play With My Hair...

I Can Sing A Song...

I Can Wait For The Sun...

I Can Be A Friend...

I Can Think Happy Thoughts...

I Can Love...

I Can Do All
These Things and More...

Because I Am Human!

Isn't It
Great To Be Human?

What Other
Special Things
Can You Think Of?

The Beginning